ANT FARMERS

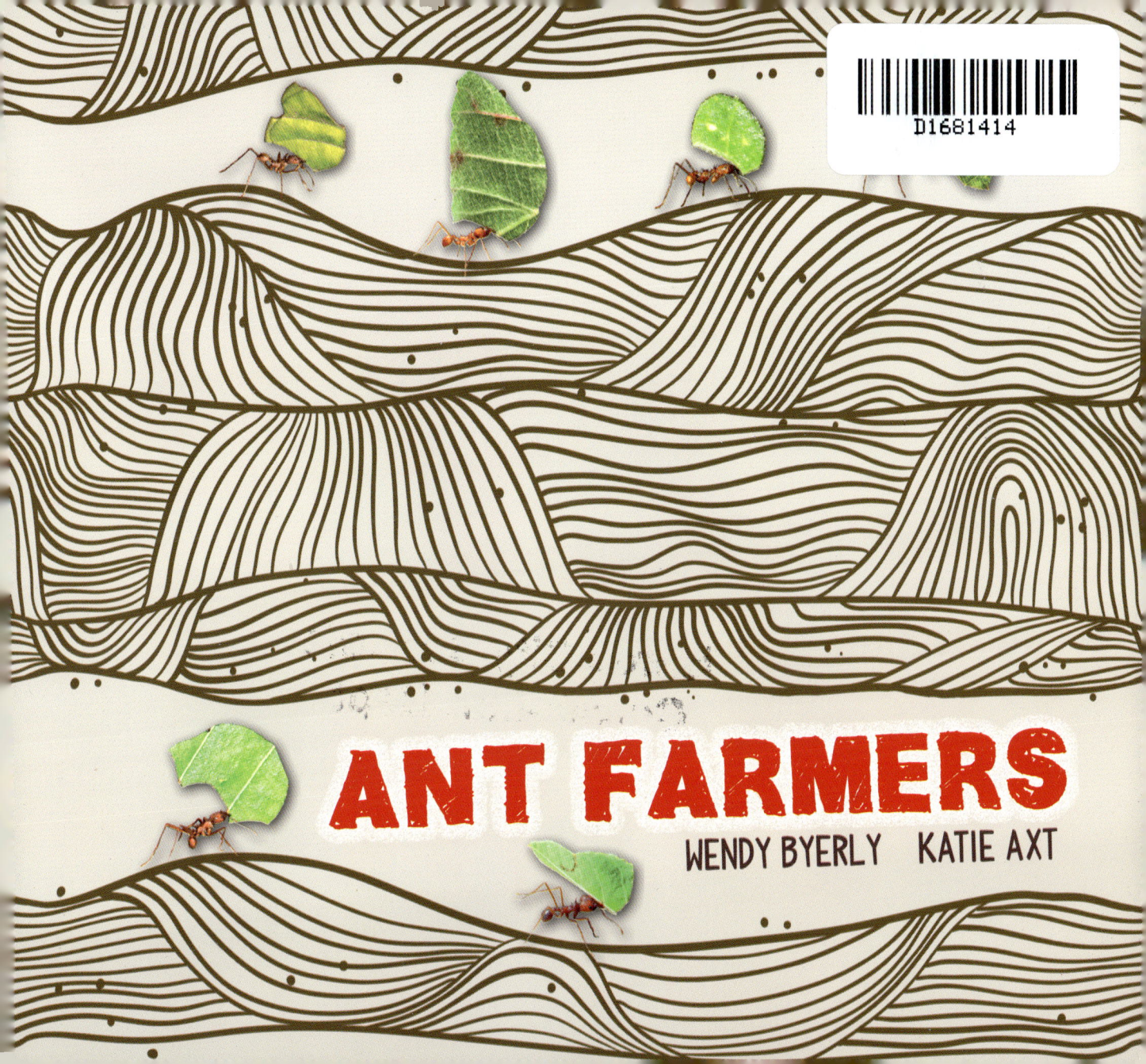

WENDY BYERLY   KATIE AXT

This is a farm.

This is a farmer.

This is an ant. This ant is a farmer, too.

All the farmer ants are girls.

This is mold.

Ants grow mold on their farms.

The mold is food for the ants to eat.

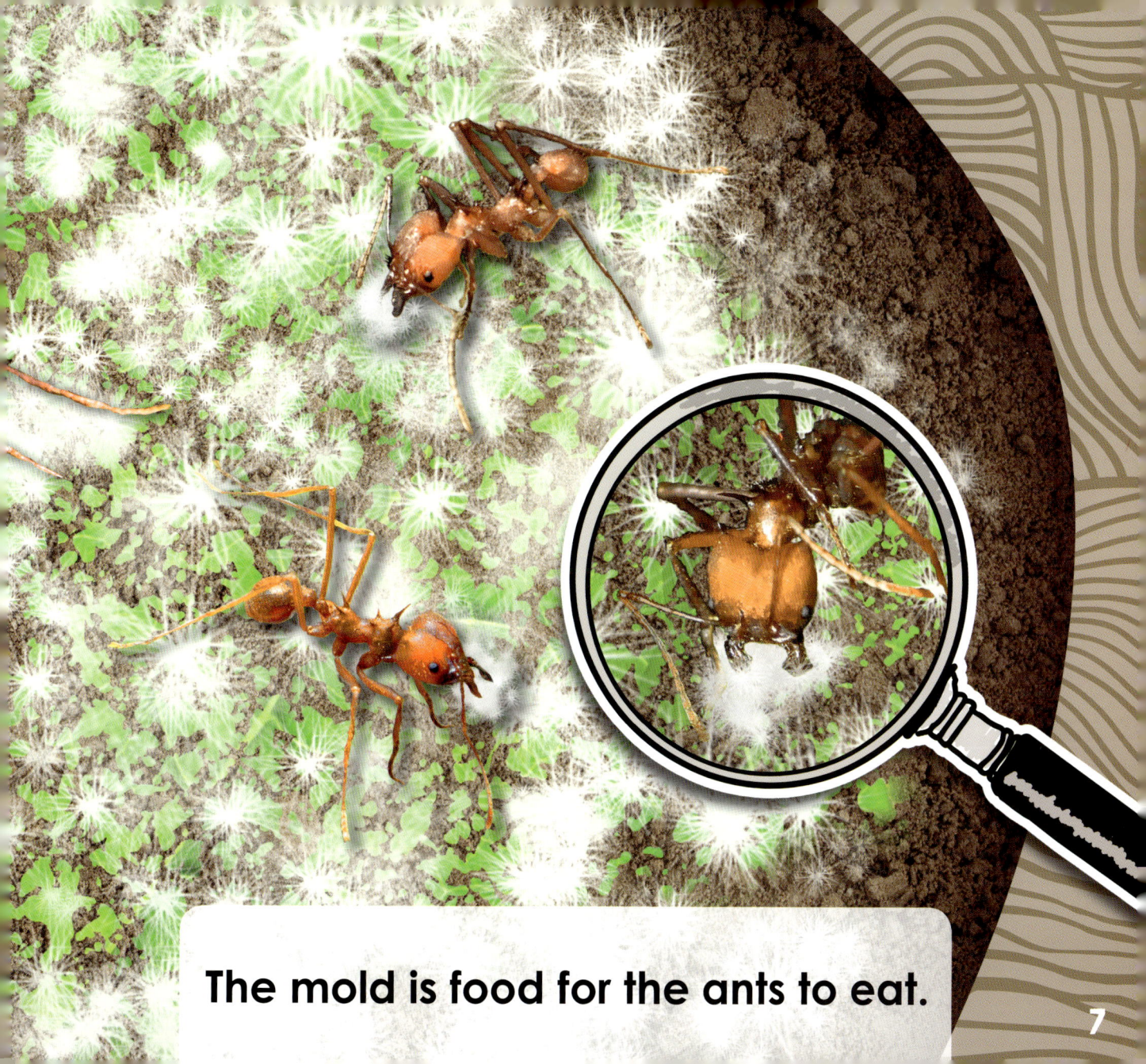

THIS IS HOW THE ANTS GROW MOLD.

The ants feed the mold leaves.

They only feed the mold leaves it likes.

First, they lick the leaves to get off the dirt.

Second, they chew up the leaves.

Then, they spit the leaves out.

GOOD MOLD

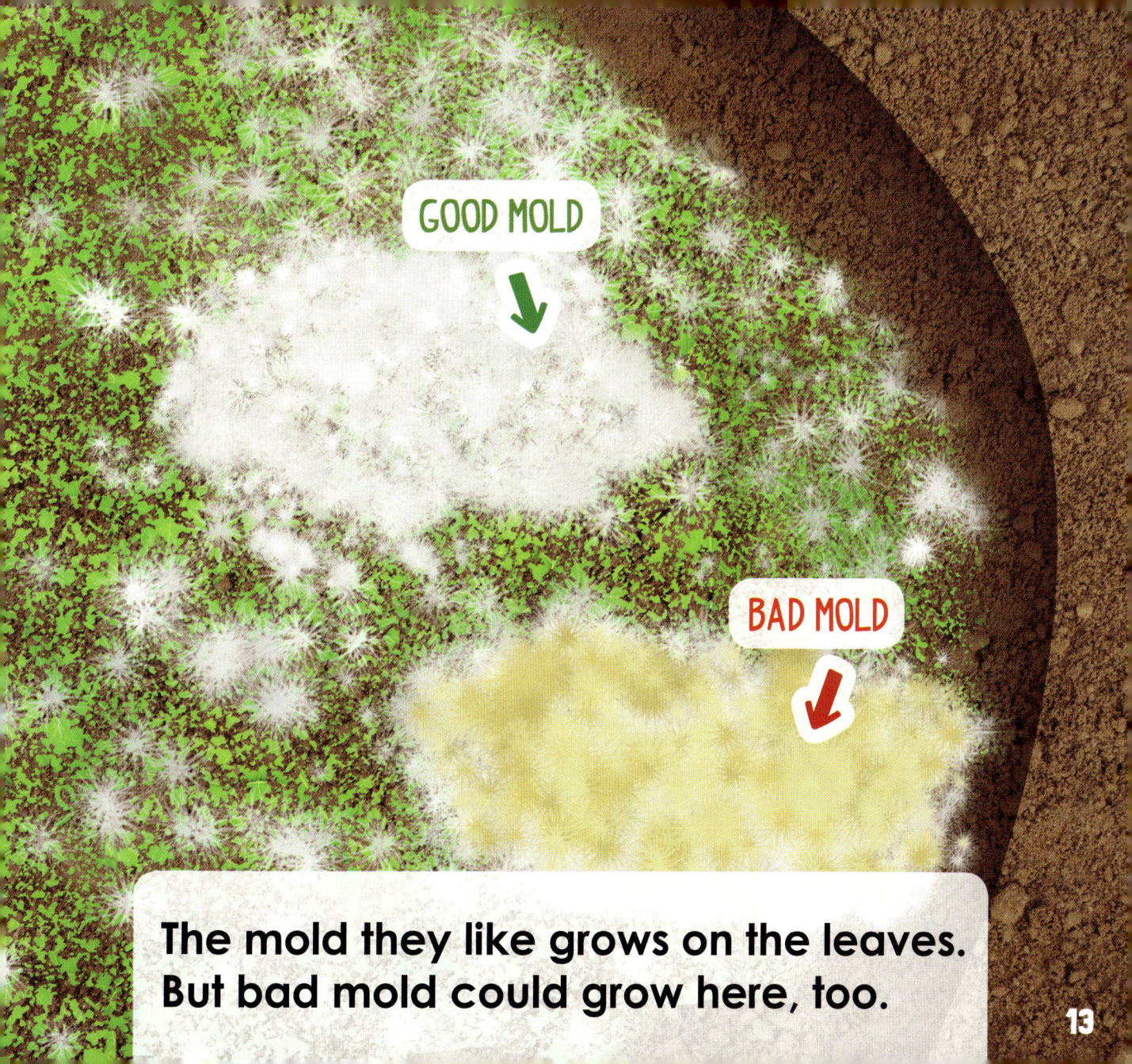

BAD MOLD

The mold they like grows on the leaves. But bad mold could grow here, too.

13

The ants mix the leaves with their poop.

Their poop helps kill the bad mold.

The ants pull out the bad mold.

They put the bad mold in the trash.

To make more mold, the ants move good mold to new spots in their nest.

If the mold starts to die, the ants start a new farm.

ANT BABY

When the mold is grown, the ants eat it. They feed it to their babies.

20

The ants can't live without the mold.
The mold can't live without the ants.
They need each other.

WORD ATTACK STRATEGIES
TIPS FOR TRICKY WORDS

Stop	**Stop** if something doesn't look right, sound right, or make sense.
	Look at the **picture**.
s___	Say the **first letter** sound.
sp___	**Blend:** Say the first two letters.
⬅	**Reread:** Go back and try again.
▢ it	**Cover** part of the word.
sp⃝it	**Chunk:** Look for parts you know.
make take	Think of a word that looks the same and **rhymes**.
blank ↩	Say **"blank,"** read on and come back.
a e i o u	Try a **different sound** for the vowel.

USING WORDS YOU KNOW
TO READ NEW WORDS

an	**it**	**not**	**see**	**will**
fan	fit	hot	seed	fill
ant	hit	spot	need	bill
ants	spit	spots	feed	kill

TRICKY WORDS

first　help　only　other　pull　their

LEAFCUTTER ANT FACTS

A leafcutter ant colony can contain over 5 million ants.

Leafcutter ants live in tropical areas of South and Central America, Mexico, and in the southern United States.

In the United States, these ants can be found in Texas, Louisiana, Florida, the Carolinas, and even New Jersey.

Leafcutter ants especially like leaves from lemon and orange trees.

These ants can carry up to 50 times their own body weight.

The mold grown by the ants is rich in nutrients and gives energy to the ants. The mold can't grow without the ants.

A leafcutter ant colony is made up of one or more queens, worker ants, eggs, and baby ants.